Management Coaching: Coaching Employees For High Performance

SADANAND PUJARI

Published by SADANAND PUJARI, 2024.

Table of Contents

Copyright

Management Coaching: Coaching Employees For High Performance

Management Coaching And Communication Book, That Enables Any Manager To Achieve Better Employee & Team Performance

First Edition: Jun 2024

Book Design by **SADANAND PUJARI**

About

Welcome to the world of management coaching. It's a $3 billion global business where the median rate for executive coaches is $500 an hour.

The news gets even better. You can be a management coach from wherever you are. I have worked with clients throughout North America, the UK, France, Switzerland, Germany, and Denmark. So can you. With technologies such as Zoom or Skype, your home office is your gateway to the world. Payments are made electronically, instantly, and easily.

Your business goals could be the same as mine: I work from where I want, with who I want, when I want, and how I want. Leaders want to get better. The competition for great executive positions is getting tighter. Those who have greater insight, knowledge, and information have an important edge over others in their industry.

To be sure, your clients want to hear about your experiences, your knowledge, your beliefs and get your advice. But the best way to serve them is to help them reach their own conclusions about how to excel as a top executive. You do this by asking really smart, thoughtful, insightful, and challenging questions. I will give you some of the most results oriented questions that I've used with my clients. But don't stop there. After your client answers your question, ask a probing follow up question. Encourage them to go even deeper.

Are you a business specialist? No problem. Your expertise in HR, technology, marketing, investor relations will serve to help specific clients see what's possible in their careers. Take me for example. I help clients who are smart, talented, and experienced but have a hard time communicating their ideas in certain business situations. That hurts their careers and the company's bottom line. I give them the communications tools they need and the confidence to succeed.

General business help is invaluable, too. You see the bigger picture and help your clients make the right moves. What about you? We tend to take for granted what we know. Don't make that assumption. Your knowledge, experience, success, and even your mistakes could prove to be a valuable resource for those that you serve.

Who are your potential clients? They could be individuals who know they need to get a leg up in order to get to the next step in their careers. You could get a portfolio of corporate clients who know that they have several members of their team who need your services. They may hire you on a monthly retainer basis.

Introduction

Imagine yourself as a top management consultant working with successful executives all over the globe and being able to do it from home. You have a lifetime of experiences. These experiences can be used to coach and help managers and executives all over the globe.

How can you maximize their talents, their potential and their experience to benefit the company, your customers, the marketplace? Well, you could tell them what to do. And sometimes you need to. Sometimes you have to say to, hey, Charlie, you need to do this or stop doing that. But the best way to get the most out of them is to ask really smart, insightful, thought provoking questions when you tell them what to do. And sometimes, as I said, you need to do that. You should do that. And sometimes you need to tell them some hard truth that maybe only you can do when you tell them what to do. They may be paying attention to you. May not be maybe their minds are elsewhere. Maybe they're secretly disagreeing with you, but they don't have the courage or whatever to speak up and tell.

You know, I think you're wrong, boss, but when you ask a question, they have no choice but to answer it, at least in their own mind. And that starts the process of creating something great. It begins to find solutions to some of the biggest problems facing your company. It begins the creative process and they are engaged. They're taking ownership of the problem and the solution. So you not only ask, by the way, great questions, but even better follow up questions, get them thinking even more. So what are the results? What results? Number one is that you have an engaged workforce. You have people that are part of you, part of the program, part of the company in ways that you never imagine.

They'll have no desire to leave your company to go elsewhere. They'll find solutions. They'll find ways of engaging your customers, of selling more products or more services to expand your marketplace by again asking really smart, really interesting, really thought provoking questions. And even better, follow up questions. I'm going to share with you some of the questions that I've shared with some of the top CEOs around the world. They're yours. If you take this Book, I promise you you're going to learn an awful lot and it will help you help your employees, help your customers, help your business. So please do join me. Some great questions are coming up in the next segment.

What Would You Do If You Weren't Afraid To Fail?

What would you do if you weren't afraid to fail, that's one of my favorite questions to ask a client, because why? It stimulates thinking. It gets us beyond our fears. It's not like you couldn't fail. Of course you could fail. But if you were putting the fear aside, it's the fear that stops us from doing what we want to do, doing what we have to do, starting new projects, creating a new business, initiating an important goal. It's the fear of failure that holds us back without that fear. Imagine what you could accomplish. Again, I find questions really important. I'm not saying that when you tell somebody to do something, it's not a good thing to do. Sometimes you have to do that.

Sometimes it's really important to give them the kind of advice that's necessary in that moment or to stop them from doing something that's destructive for them or for others. But that's passive communication when you tell somebody to do something. But when you ask them to do something, when you ask them to think about something that is active communication, it forces us to think, to see what's possible, to illuminate what could be, to examine how we could move things forward with fresh thinking, how we could invent or create something new. That's why I love questions so much. And when you eliminate the fear of failure, imagine what you could get done.

What If A Hot Shot Took Over My Job?

A business executive by the name of Kat Cole came up with something she calls her hot shot questions. Now, they're great questions for your people. If you're an executive coach or you're a business owner or you're a business leader within your company, or here's a concept. You could ask these questions to yourself, no matter where you are, no matter how high up you are in the food chain in the company. So here's the Hot Shot questions. If a hot shot came in and took over your job, what's the first change they would make? What's the second change?

How about a third change? And here's the follow up. Why can't I make those changes? What's stopping me from making those changes? Why do I love these questions? They again, stir our creativity, see what else is possible, see what else we could do to make ourselves better, to make the company better, to delight our customers. What would a hot shot do? Who came from the outside, took over your job? And why can't you do what the Hot Shot does?

How To Be Your Own Best Coach

Now, I know this Book is about how you can be a great business coach if you're an executive at a company or you own the company, but I come from the assumption that we know ourselves better than anybody else in the world. So that's why I find this an interesting question. So here, if you're a boss, you can ask somebody on your team this question. If you were your own business coach, what advice would you be giving yourself?

Why do I like that question? Again, it asks the employee to start taking a hard look at who they are, how they could be better, how they could be then at their best selves, how could they be the best sales executive marketing director, whatever their job is? How could they be the best at what they are, at what they could be. And whatever answer they give you says to them, that's interesting.

So what's holding you back from being you at your best as a sales executive and marketing director? And what steps could you advise yourself to take to get to where you could be, where you know you should be in your job and in your career? And again, they're giving themselves advice. It's far more powerful in many ways than you telling them what to do. How would you feel if you were the best salesperson you possibly could be?

What would that look like? How much more effective would you be at your job if you were at your best? And again, it excites them. They're seeing new possibilities. They're imagining themselves in a new, different and better place. And they're also laying out the steps they can take to get to where they want to be tried out with your people. Ask them if you were your own business coach, what advice would you give you so you could be even better at what you do?

Can We Truly Change Our Behavior?

Is change possible? Can we alter a lifetime pattern of self-destructive behavior or unkindness to others messing up our lives, our careers? Is that change possible? Well, I certainly hope it is. If not, then why are we in the coaching business? My firm belief is that we are most open to changing our lives when we are in the greatest amount of pain, when we have hit rock bottom in our careers and in our lives. This is true of people with addiction problems, people who have messed up what should otherwise have been a great career, people who have spent a ridiculous amount of money and now they're broken on and on and on by self-defeating behavior.

When we feel that pain, when we truly see how we are responsible for what is going on in our lives, then as coaches we can move in and truly give them some outstanding advice and help them be on the path of redemption and goodness. It's not to say that people aren't open to good ideas or they can't see better ways of living. Their lives are doing more effective work at the job. They certainly could do that without feeling pain. I'm just saying that when they are most open to it is when things look bleak, when they feel something different. So be prepared to point out how they are screwing things up and when they realize it, when they truly feel it, then as a coach, you can move in and help them to have a new and better life.

Don't Be A Prisoner Of Perfectionism

Don't be a prisoner of perfectionism, what do I mean by that? We all want to be perfect, but frankly, none of us are perfect and rarely is anything we do in life or in work perfect. Our goal should not be perfect, but our goal should be excellence. Really, really, really good. When you strive for perfectionism, you spend so much time and effort making it exactly perfect that you ignore other facets of your business and of your life. And so, again, my suggestion is go for being great, not perfect. Your job as a coach is to suggest ways that your clients can see not perfectionism, but new possibilities for their lives and for their careers, new ways of doing things, alternatives to what they've been doing in the past or even today. That is a much better goal than perfectionism. There's that old expression which I like a lot. Don't let the perfect be the enemy of the good.

What's The One Goal You Could Complete That Would Make Your

Here's the question I think all bosses should ask all their employees, even their high performing people, is there one thing, just one thing you could do to be even better at your job? Now, why do I like this question? Number one is it's not overwhelming. I'm not telling you to come up with 10 things or 15 things or 20 things to be better. Just one thing, one thing at a time. It's not overwhelming. It's not. Oh, my God. I don't know if I could do all those things. You're focusing on one thing at a time. It's like bite size pieces of getting better at your job and all of us can be better. So even the people who you think are the best in your company, even they could use improvement.

And again, when they come up with their own answer about the one thing they can do to be even better at whatever they do, they're empowering themselves. They're coming up with their answers, not yours. I think it's exciting. I think people will feel encouraged to take on one task at a time to get better without the feeling that they've got a mountain of things they've got to do to get better. So try it with you people, all of them, those who need a lot of help and those who are even your top people. See what the results are. I think you'd be surprised.

What Are Your Three Greatest Achievements In Business?

Which Litvin is one of the best coaches around? I read his books, I read his blogs, I read his chapters, he's just a really smart guy. He co-authored a book called The Prospero's Coach. I think you're going to get a lot out of it. I certainly have. And it's really worth reading, which came up with what he calls his one hundred and twenty one great coaching questions. And they really are terrific. I'm not going to give you all a hundred and twenty one. I've distilled down what I would consider the most important to what we're talking about, how to be a great executive coach, how to get the best out of your people, how to raise the game of your employees and your own game too. So here's Rich's first question.

What are your three greatest business successes, your three greatest career achievements? What impact did you make? What income did you create? What difference did you make in the company, in your customers' lives, in your lives, in the world's existence? What are your three greatest achievements now? Rich believes that most of us are going to have a hard time. We're going to be hard pressed to come up with three great achievements. My belief is maybe even if we could. My belief is that we are more likely to know our three biggest failures in business, our three biggest mistakes in our careers.

And why I think that's important is we do not give ourselves credit for the good things we've done or are doing now. We're more likely to keep replaying. We have nightmares of our full pause in business and in our careers. And when you focus on what you've achieved, when you concentrate on all the good things that you've done, it gives you positive reinforcement, encourages you to do more great things. Now, I'm not saying you should ignore your mistakes. You should acknowledge them for sure and learn from them. But don't dwell on them. Focus on what you've done well and the impact those achievements made on your life and the lives of others.

What Would You Sacrifice To Achieve Your Goals

Here are a couple of more questions from Rich Litvin. One hundred and twenty one questions to be a great coach, what would you be willing to sacrifice to reach your goals? And the other question is the other side of the same coin. What would you willing not to sacrifice to get what you want to reach your goals? Well, here's my take here. Here are my answers to that question. To me, the greatest investment you could make to get what you want in business and in life is time and effort. Take the time to be as knowledgeable to find the right path to getting what you want. So, for example, if you want to be a great executive coach, I hope this Book is helping you. I truly do. But we need other great books on coaching from people whose reputation is sterling. Find out from those that you trust who are the best in the business in terms of teaching me how to be an outstanding coach.

Watch YouTube videos again, the same kinds of quality people who can give you great information, stuff that you're not going to just find anywhere but through experience, knowledge and know-how. What would you do not to get what you want? What would you not sacrifice? I hope it's not your integrity, not your honesty, not who you are, what you stand for. It's easy to cut corners and think this is the way to do it, or to cheat or to lie and to fool people that you've achieved your goals. That's what you do not want to sacrifice your integrity, who you are, what you stand for and what you believe in. Those are my thoughts on this. I'd like to hear from you.

What's The One Thing You Can Do To Be Better At Anything?

Let's say you were to make a list of all of your goals in business, I don't care how long the list is, three, four or five, one hundred goals. Doesn't matter if you were to focus on one goal to the exclusion of the others. Just really focus on one goal, the one goal that you would think would be the most likely to achieve, the most likely to make happen, the one that would come to fruition. Which goal would it be?

Let me add a few other layers to this question. Why would it be so important for you to achieve this goal? How would your life be different? How would your business be more successful? How would you feel better, happier, healthier? How would others be in a better place if you achieved this goal? Why is it so important? How is your life and your business different?

My belief is, is that when you understand why this is so important really emphasized, why is this so important? And it is clear in your mind why it's so important and the obstacles that you may have and there will be will not be so insurmountable. You will be more motivated, more energized, more focused on accomplishing that goal.

What Are You Not Paying Attention To And What Is It Costing You?

This is a question that every boss, every business owner, every executive must ask all of their key employees ready? What are you not paying attention to? What's going on in our industry, in our business, with our competition in the world, with culture, with politics that we are oblivious to? And how is that affecting our profits, our business expansion, our service to our customers and understanding what our customers want, what they're looking for and how their tastes may have changed over the years? Why are we not paying attention to them? Let me give you a couple of examples. The dairy industry was not paying attention to millions of their customers looking for alternative products to stuff that comes out of a cow. So their customers were drinking almond milk or oat milk and not the traditional kind of milk. The results, two of the biggest dairies in the United States went out of business, gone forever because they were not paying attention to their customers.

Every car company or virtually every car company is playing catch up. Now to who? To Tesla. Why didn't they see that car buyers around the world were interested in alternative vehicles such as EVs, electric vehicles? Tesla got it. They got it years ago. And so GM, Ford, Volkswagen, Chrysler, Mercedes, they're all playing catch up to Tesla and it's costing them a lot of money. And their customers are looking elsewhere to buy new cars. So the question, again, you have for your people is, what are you not paying attention to? What are our blind spots in our business? How do we open our eyes and open our minds to the changes going on in the world, which are incredibly fast and furious that we need to be aware of? What are we not paying attention to?

Pay Attention In Your Personal Life

The same two words of advice in our personal lives. Pay attention. I would make the argument that a lot of marriages, relationships end because one or both of the partners were not paying attention. They were not listening to the signals. They're not hearing the tone of the voice of their loved one, the anguish, the depression, the anger. They weren't paying attention. Same thing. When it comes to parents, somehow their kids are someplace else. They're not paying attention.

Most of the mistakes or accidents in our lives are happening because, again, our heads are someplace else. Our focus is someplace else. We're not paying attention. Driving our cars, accidents, traffic tickets, summonses for disobeying highway laws are happening because we're not paying attention. If you don't pay attention to the lives of you and your loved ones, you risk going down a road that you'll regret for the rest of your lives. So please pay attention.

How Did You Become Great And How Could You Mess It Up?

Let's say you have an employee that's doing really, really well, that's great, that's a good thing. It's good for you. It's a good thing for your employee. It's good for everybody. So the questions you might want to ask that individual are how did you get to where you are today? What steps did you take to become a great sales executive, for example? What changes and what adjustments did you make? What plans did you have and act? What new ideas did you come up with? Why are those questions important? They reinforce in your successful employees mind what they did well and how they used those steps to get to where they are today. Again, it's not you telling them how they got to where they are. It's them telling themselves much more powerful, more impactful, more positive reinforcement that they're giving themselves. And indirectly, Of course, from you, too. Now, here's a kind of an interesting follow up question.

A little provocative, a little edgy, but here goes, OK, if you were to screw this up, if you were to really self sabotage and so if you were to mess this up. What would you do now? Probably they're not going to do it, but they need to be aware of that. Damage could happen, bad things could happen, and when your awareness is heightened, when your radar is a lot sharper to what could go wrong, you are in a better position to avoid any pitfalls that might hinder the successful achievements that you have enacted. Why have you gotten good at what you do? How did you do it? What steps did you take? What adjustments did you make? And how could you screw it up? Both very important types of questions that will help your employees be great, remain great. And avoid messing things up.

What Happens When The Stuff Hits The Fan?

One of the biggest challenges you'll ever have as a coach is getting the people that you serve to take responsibility when things go wrong. Our natural tendency is to blame anything and everything except ourselves. Oh, it was covid-19 and it was the worst economic downturn since the Great Depression. All of which, by the way, are true. Nobody can deny the reality of what was going on in the world. The question is, what did you do to adjust to change your style, your strategy, your tactics in light of what was happening? Or maybe how could you benefit, given the situation that was going on in the world? Certainly, folks who made hand sanitizers and masks figured out a way of making a lot of money and helping a lot of people at the same time during the height of the situation. Let me use myself as an example. When the shutdown first hit, I thought to myself, well, this could be a challenging year.

I, generally speaking, meet with my coaching clients or the groups that I do communications training with in person. And that's great. But obviously during the shutdown, I could not do it. So what did I do? I used Skype. I used Zoome. I used Microsoft's version of WebEx, anything, any modality where I could communicate with people, either one on one or two groups doing training around the world. I was working with clients in Europe, in Asia, everywhere else in North America. It was exciting for me and it was helpful and productive for those that I served. So I figured out a way to adjust to what was going on in the world. So help your clients to see how they are responsible for their own success or failures. When they take responsibility, they can say, OK, now what? What do I do now? What's the solution? And by the way, when they succeed, they'll feel much better about themselves because they know that they're in charge of their own lives and their own success.

What Advice Would You Give The Ten Year Old Version Of You?

Here's a question I'd love to ask clients: what advice would you give the 10 year old version of you? And one client gave me some interesting answers. He said, well, I would tell that person to study harder, to work harder, to save more money later on in life when you're working, put aside at least 10 percent of your income and save it for a rainy day. And here's the best piece of advice I would give. The younger version of me is nicer to people, especially those who are not perhaps quite unquote on your level, like a waiter or waitress, the door man. And you're building people who don't have your income, don't have your status or prestige, be nicer to them.

So that's pretty good advice. I think the second follow up question is, are you doing that now as a mature, probably fairly accomplished adult? And more often than not, they all say they need improvement in that area. It reminds everybody who they are, what they stand for, what they believe in, and what constitutes good behavior. The advice you gave that 10 year old version of you is something that you need to follow as an adult.

How To Be Better, Smarter, And Richer

There's a process that I love to do with corporations, corporate clients of mine, it's called better, smarter, richer. I tell them to gather groups of five to eight employees, and then I ask each group a series of very provocative, interesting questions, such as, what do you wish people knew about us that they don't? Or conversely, what's the biggest misconception others have about our company and whatever they say? And they're going to come up with a lot of great insights and great observations about that you could follow. OK, so how do we clarify who we are, what we stand for, what we believe, and how do we get rid of all those misconceptions? And they'll come up with even more interesting ideas. How can we better serve our customers again? You're going to hear five to eight great ideas, maybe even more than that.

Maybe we'll combine some ideas that we've heard. Maybe somebody will hear that idea and that will spark something new in their thinking. So my follow up question is great ideas, folks. Now, what do we do starting tomorrow? What are the three ways we can serve our customers better based on what we talked about here and now, what are our competitors doing that maybe we should think about doing, you know, sometimes the competition as an idea that we can, how shall we say, borrow again? What can we do starting tomorrow, starting Monday, whenever that will help us do that? Where are we wasting money now? I have to tell you, sometimes the best thinking about that comes from folks who are sort of lower on the corporate totem pole, the receptionist, some of the younger associates they're seeing where money is wasted, sometimes more than the folks who are in the C suite.

So make sure you get ideas from everybody. Where could we spend more money? Where should we be using our resources more productively, more intelligently? Again, these ideas will flow and it will generate all kinds of exciting, innovative ways of running the company. But again, always the follow up question is great. Starting tomorrow, what steps can we take to be wiser about the way we allocate our resources? Great ideas are meaningless without taking concrete steps.

Three Reasons You Are Not Reaching Your Goals

Here's a great coaching question: what are the three reasons you have not achieved your goals or put it another? Right. What are the three reasons you are not where you expected to be either in your life? Or in your business, the belief is that we are responsible for our success, so if we're not where we want to be, if we're not getting our goals accomplished, that we must be doing something to stop ourselves from getting where we want to be. So what are the three reasons? Everybody has their reasons. Here's what I hear a lot from my clients, and I thought I'd pass them on to you. Number one is a lack of commitment if you want to lose 50 pounds.

Hey, great. What are you going to do about it? What is your food plan and how are you going to stick to it if you're going to also set up an exercise program? Are you going to do it at least five days a week, four days a week? Whatever it is, you need to do it on a regular basis. It takes a plan and it takes a commitment and a strong reason why you must achieve that goal. Perhaps it's a health reason. Perhaps the way you look, your self-esteem, whatever it is, you have to have that compelling reason in order to succeed. Number two, what I hear a lot is a lack of grit. What do I mean by grit? Grit is resilience.

When you get knocked on your rear end, when you fail, when you make a big mistake, when somebody says no to you, do you have the grit or the resilience to get back on your feet and move forward to achieve those goals or the success that you're looking for? Now, the smartest thing to do is to learn why I failed. Why did I make the mistake? What can I learn from those incidents that will help me to be successful in my next effort and be smart about it? But again, grit is about, again, results. We're all going to make mistakes. We're all going to get setbacks. We're all going to fail at some time. The question is, what do you do after that? Number three is an interesting one.

If you want to achieve something that's really important to you, a goal or a job or whatever it is, are you doing it for you? Or are you doing it for the approval of somebody else or the fear of their disapproval, if it's about the approval, the good opinion of others? You'll never feel good about yourself, even if you achieve your goals and somehow or another you'll feel a little empty, a little hollow, you may even sabotage yourself on the way to trying to be successful in whatever you're trying to do, because why? It's not yours. You don't own it.

Somebody else owns it. And in effect, they own you. When you are trying to get the approval of someone else, you are, in effect, their prisoners. So please make sure this is important to you. Make sure you are owning the process and the achievement. And it's not for anybody else. It is for you. Those are three reasons that I'm told a lot in my practice. I'd love to hear from you. What are people telling you that's stopping them from achieving their goals or getting what they want out of life or work? Maybe you could also share some of what stops you.

How Overcoming Obstacles Can Give The Confidence To Achieve Anything

Have you ever had to overcome a substantial obstacle in your career in order to be successful? The reason I like this question is because it happens to all of us. At some point we reach a wall. Sometimes it's self-imposed, sometimes it comes from outside. But we reach that place where we say if we don't somehow or another get beyond this, we'll never be successful. And it certainly happened to me when I was a young reporter with the Associated Press radio network. I was good at getting the story. I was a good journalist. I could write the story well, report well, and broadcast it, but I was not good at the technical aspects of the job, the editing, the producing, things like that. And the boss brings me into his office, says, you're a great reporter. You're not good at the technical part of the job and you've got to figure that out.

If you don't, we're going to have to let you go. And that really shook me up. And so I took a long walk with myself. I walked the streets of Washington, D.C. for hours and hours and I said to myself, I've got to figure this out. And I found a mentor at the network and I said, please teach me how to do this. And he did. And I practiced and I practiced. I practiced and I got it right. I went on to have a great career in journalism. Now, it also gave me the self-confidence to know that when bad stuff happens, when I reach a wall, an obstacle, I can figure it out. A related question that I like. It's perhaps a more positive question.

Was there a turning point in your life and your career that has helped you to find success going forward? And some woman once said she climbed Mount Kilimanjaro. She never thought she could do it, but she did it. A guy said he was the captain of his college basketball team and it gave him leadership skills which helped him in business in the future. So, again, these questions remind ourselves of what we can do, how we can overcome adversity, how we can tap into things that we've done, experiences we've had in our life, in our career that can help us go beyond what we ever thought we could do.

Great Coaches Teach The Power Of Empathy

There is nothing more important that you can teach somebody you're working with than the power of empathy. Empathy is about understanding where others are coming from, what they care about, what their fears and anxieties are, their hopes and their dreams. You make that empathetic connection by asking really smart, incisive questions, things like what do you wish people knew about you that they don't know?

What's the biggest misconception folks might have about you? Again, you're seeing where they are coming from. Empathy does not necessarily mean agreement. You can understand what their beliefs are. That doesn't necessarily mean that you are in accord with them. You encourage people to open up with more by nodding your head or taking notes.

Now, if they say something that you profoundly disagree with, don't nod your head, just remain neutral. Again, empathy is about seeing the perspective, the point of view of others. It is vitally important in coaching. It's extremely important in sales and marketing. Is empathy a powerful tool that we all must have?

Great Coaches Know How To Persuade Anybody To Do What's

We make the vast majority of our decisions based more on how we feel about something than what we think about something. Let me give you some examples. We all wear clothes, right? The good reasons, the rational reasons, the cognitive reasons of why we wear clothes, well, they protect us against the elements. If it's cold or rainy or snowy, we wear clothes to protect us from the bad weather. And that's all good and all correct. We also have a social contract. We don't leave our homes naked again. It's irrational, correct reasons for why we wear clothes. But if those were the only reasons why we would buy clothes, we can get the least expensive clothes that would protect us against the elements and shield our modesty and not spend a lot of money on clothing.

But let's be honest, we spend an inordinate amount of money based on how clothes make us feel, how they make us look, the message it sends to others. I'm powerful, I'm sexy, artsy, whatever the emotional attachment is that we give to clothes. Same thing when it comes to cars. If you have two cars driven by two drivers at Point A and they need to go to point B, one is the world's most expensive car and the other is the cheapest car. But their goal is to get to point B that no matter how expensive or cheap the car is, they'll both fulfill the job of getting you where you want to be. Will one be more comfortable? Would be a better looking car. Will one send a message to those who are looking at you driving that car? You're powerful, you're rich, you've made it big time.

Yeah, probably it will. But again, the basic function of the car is the same thing with a home. We tend to get a home that again, makes us feel good, makes us feel comfortable. What I am saying is that if you want to persuade anyone, go for how they feel about something rather than what they think about it, get out of their rational space and get into their emotional place. That's really true when it comes to sales. It certainly is true when it comes to networking. And it's absolutely true if you want to persuade somebody to do something important.

The Three Most Powerful Words In Persuasion

Here are the three most powerful words in networking ready? Here's what's possible when you are reaching out to somebody as a potential networking partner, you want to show them that by combining forces, both of you could have a better tomorrow, a more positive future than what you have separately today. Here's what's possible. Engages the imagination. It sees something that could be. And by the way, imagine is another very powerful word. If you start a sentence with imagine if we combine forces, your knowledge of technology, my ability in the world of marketing. Imagine what we could accomplish as a team together, how we could make incredible connections for the future. Imagine here's what's possible.

Or what if phrases and words that again connect us to a better tomorrow, a better future for both of us. Here's what persuasion either in networking or anything else should never be. It should never be about pressuring anybody. It shouldn't be about strongly arming them or cajoling them. If you have to do that, then they're wondering to themselves, why should I do this? What does this person really offer me instead? Here's what's possible. Talks about something better for both of you in the future.

How To Help Someone Achieve The Most Important Goal In Their Lives

Go small or go home. Yes, I realize the expression is go big or go home. But when it comes to tackling a major life altering goal, going small, that is taking small, gradual steps may be the best way to go. So, for example, let's say you're working with somebody who wants to lose a tremendous amount of weight. Let's say it's one hundred pounds. Instead of saying you have got to dramatically and drastically change the way you eat, you have to start working out two hours a day. If you really want to achieve that goal, they are going to resist it. They're going to push back. They're just not going to do it. So the best way is what are the three smallest steps we can do every single day to help us make that goal. So, for example, let's say the person you're working with drinks three liters a day of Coca-Cola.

That's a lot of sugar and it's like a hundred snicker bars or something like that. Say to them, OK, just starting this week, let's say you drank only two liters of Coca-Cola a day. And the week after that, it's one liter of Coca-Cola a day. You're going to gradually, slowly change their behavior instead of working at two hours a day. Let's say it was 15 minutes a day of working out the first week, then increase it to twenty minutes, twenty five minutes, etc., every ensuing week thereafter. So it's a gradual change. It's a gradual shift in perception and habits. So it's not some mountain you have to climb. It's a gradual increase of your effort toward reaching your goal.

It's Not What You Say, It's What They Hear

It's not what you say, it's what they hear. One of the biggest mistakes we make in communications is the assumption that people understand us, that we're being so clear to them. And it's really a mistake that most of us make in our own lives. I don't know about you. I wake up early in the morning, I go to the kitchen, I turn the coffee on, I feed my pets. And I'm also beginning that inner conversation with myself. And I have to tell you folks, I speak fluently. I understand myself perfectly. And that inner dialogue does not end until I go to sleep later that night. My guess is right now you're talking to yourself even as you're listening to me again, because I understand myself so well, I could make the critical error.

And it would be a very critical error in thinking that therefore, everybody else understands me. My wife and I have been together for over twenty six years and we have the kind of relationship where we can practically finish each other's sentences. That said, there are times that I've said things to Susan that I thought I was being clear about, but she did not understand and vice versa, that now we have a close, intimate relationship, to say the least. But in the world of networking, business, sales, even your personal life, it's quite possible you're dealing with strangers. And so therefore, what do you need to do? You need to take extra steps to make sure that whatever you're saying is as clear as it possibly can be.

So whenever you say something that's pretty important, pretty meaningful, follow it up with phrases such as yours. What I mean by that, here's an example of what I'm talking about. Here's how I came to this conclusion. Here are the implications of what I'm suggesting here. Here's how this might impact or benefit you in some meaningful way. In other words, again, what I'm doing is I'm just not stopping. And what I said, I'm taking extra steps to ensure to the best of my abilities that you understand what I mean. Give it a try.

Help Your Clients To Be Powerful Communicators

One of the most important jobs we have as a coach is to help our clients to communicate clearly, persuasively and productively. Let me give you a statistic that I find incredible. 90 percent of our conversations are with ourselves, 90 percent from the moment that I wake up in the morning. I'm having this internal dialogue with me until I go to bed later that night. Now I understand myself perfectly.

The mistake that I would make and we all would make is the assumption that everybody else understands us. So to that end of being as clear as we possibly could be, we always must translate and interpret what we mean. Here's what I mean by that. Here's what I'm talking about. Here's an example of what I mean.

Here are the implications of what I'm talking about. Here's how I came to this conclusion. Here's my thinking about this subject. In other words, you're always clarifying what you mean. So those that you were talking about to the best of their ability, get what you mean.

Great Coaches Help Clients To Be Effective Listeners

There is nothing more important for a coach than to help the person that he or she is working with, to be a great listener, to really understand what is being said, what is being asked of them, what would success look like?

How do they go about accomplishing what the speaker is asking them to do? Could they get examples of what the speaker is talking about? The whole goal is clarity to make sure that the one who is listening truly understands what's being said is their emotion and emphasis on certain words, certain phrases, certain sentences, which again, would give the listener a better idea of where things need to go and how they need to accomplish what is being asked of them.

Listen, really, really listen. Just don't parrot back words. Make sure you understand the intent of what is being asked of you.

Coach Clients To Use The Power Of Their Voice

Virtually all of us have this incredibly powerful instrument within our body that helps us to become even better communicators, it is our voice. Our voice can communicate passion, energy. It can be used to emphasize points. You remember some time ago, maybe even still today, we would use these yellow highlighters to highlight a certain passage on a page for us to remember later. Well, our voices can do the same thing. We can increase our energy. We can increase the volume or lower the volume or pause before we're about to make a really important point, as if we're telling the audience, hey, folks, pay attention. What I'm about to say is really, really important for you to know and for you to remember when you're in a listening mode. Listen again to the voice, the style of voice that the person who is speaking to you is using.

Again, same thing, passion, energy, volume, all things that they are conveying to you about what they believe is important for you to understand about them. Another part of our body also can be used to communicate, and that is our hands. Our hands energize our performance. At the same time, they have the wonderful quality of dissipating the nervousness that's in our bodies. So the user is energized. It'll bring your performance up and we'll also take a lot of the edge off of us that's in our body, our voice, our hands. Use them to convey even more meaning in your presentation.

How To Help Your Clients Feel Successful

What are the most painful things that any coach can hear from a client is how that person feels like a failure. They somehow or another feel that everybody else is having a great time. Everybody else is successful except them. And they tend to get these messages mainly on social media. They go to Facebook or Instagram and see how their so-called friends had this fabulous vacation, their show, all their pictures online. But forget to mention that they got food poisoning while they're on vacation or they bought this great new laptop. Oh, it's got all the bells and whistles. Except they never mentioned that they paid too much for it because they went to the wrong store.

What you see and hear in social media is filtered information from people. It is not surprising that so many others see this feel like they're failures, like they're not measuring up. Why isn't their life working out? So your job as their coach is to point out where they are successful, where they overcame tremendous odds, cleared obstacles, had turning points in their lives and in their careers that they created so they can look at their own lives without comparing themselves to anybody else and see the goodness and the gold.

How To Give A World Class Presentation

What are the most important things you can teach somebody that you're working with is how to give a great presentation? Frankly, most of the presentations that I see in business are horrible. They stink, they're boring, they're dull. They're not very productive. They're not telling me something that I have to know, something that's going to advance my cause either in business or in life. So let me give you some of my tips on how to give a great presentation. Number one is to grab the audience's attention. In most of the presentations that I see speakers back into their speech and their presentation, they see things like, oh, it's great to be here in Cleveland.

Who cares? Charlie, the person who introduced you, Charlie and I go back twenty five years, boring, uninteresting, not relevant. So instead, start with either a bold statement, a great story that is relevant to your speech or a provocative, thought provoking question. If you're asking me which one I like, I like all three. But the ones that I like the most are either the story or the question why a bold statement can be great, can really grab some attention, but it's passive communication. They may be listening. They may not be listening. Their minds may be elsewhere. You don't know. But a story when you tell that story is that they're imagining the scenario playing out in their mind. They're seeing this whole thing work out in their imagination.

A great question forces them to answer the question, at least to themselves, and they are then suddenly becoming involved in what you are talking about. And that is active communication, the story and the question. So I tend to go with that over the bold statement. But again, the bold statement can be great. If it's done really well, tell them something they don't know. A lot of speeches and presentations seem all too familiar. And once you start going over ground that has been trampled on a million times before the audience starts going elsewhere, their mind is going to what they had for breakfast that morning, what they're going to do for dinner that night, the fight they have with their spouse, whatever it is, they're not focusing on your speech. So tell them something.

Give them a wow moment where they say to themselves, wow, that's really interesting. How does it solve their problems? How do they advance their causes? How does it give them something that will either help them to be more successful in their business, their life, their health, whatever it is you're talking about, give them something that when they say to themselves, I never thought about that. That's really interesting. This person who's speaking understands my problems and has given me some ideas of how to combat the problem that I am dealing with. That's the WOW movement. And every speech has to have that wow moment.

Now, people say to me, you know, should I use PowerPoint? I'm not a big fan of PowerPoint, but because I don't think PowerPoint can't be helpful, it can be. But most of the time it's not used particularly well. It overwhelms the speech rather than supplementing it. So a good PowerPoint chapter has bold graphs that really bring to life the point you're making or a picture or something. Again, that supports what you're saying, not overwhelms a story from my own life. A client of mine was the CEO of one of the biggest insurance companies in the world, called me up and said, hey, I'm going to be in New York. I'm going to make a presentation before a lot of big investment people. Can you come and watch it and critique it for me? I said, sure.

So he gave his presentation and afterwards he said to me, So what do you think? I said, look, your chapters were so loaded with tiny little graphs, million numbers, it was impossible for me to really take them in and also listen to you. I can't do both. Maybe I'm not that smart, but either can listen to you or try to read, try to comprehend the tiny little numbers and graphs and facts that are overpopulating your chapters. So, again, fewer chapters, bolder graphs or pictures to supplement, not overwhelm your points. How do you finish your presentation? Well, some people say you should sum up what you just said for the past twenty minutes. OK, I don't mind that. That's fine if you're going to do that. But don't stop there. At The end of your speech, your presentation should be action oriented. What do you want them to do? What will get them to the place where they want to be that solves their problem that you stated earlier in the speech? Lay it out there. Step one, step two, step three. Tell them what to do. Give them the path to their success.

Tips On Getting New Coaching Clients

I'm often asked, how do I get new clients? New coaches ask me that question all the time. Well, if social media works for you, if that's the way you get the word out about what you do, great. If posting an article or an insight about coaching on LinkedIn, for example, helps to bring in possible clients, fantastic. For me, it doesn't work so well. What works for me is doing great coaching work. I am successful with my clients. They become my marketing machine. They became my PR agency. They are my advertisers. They tell everyone they know, hey, this guy did tremendous work for me. He really helped me to get what I'm looking for in business and in life. And folks that they're talking to more often than not call me up and say, can we chat now? They really don't know me.

So what do I do? I like to have a conversation with them, but it's got to be a powerful conversation. It's going to be so meaningful, so in depth, so insightful. It's something they'll never forget for the rest of their lives, something where they say to themselves, I have to work with. So I don't charge them for that. I want them to really say to themselves, I think this guy can help me. And by giving them that hour of a very powerful, very in-depth conversation, that is the best marketing tool you can possibly have beyond that word of mouth. So give it a try. Tell me what you think.

Do You Trust Your People To Work From Home?

Increasingly, people are going to be working from home, you may like that, you may not like that, but that is the reality. The question is for a coach to an executive at a company. Do you trust your people to get the work done? If you don't trust them, if you think they're spending a lot of time on YouTube or reading some other chapters or whatever and not doing the tasks at hand, the things that you are paying them to do, if they're not doing that and you don't trust them, then you did a bad job of hiring. Let me explain. You should only want people to work for you who are self starters, who don't need to be pushed or prodded or cajoled into doing what they were hired to do. If they're not doing that, if they're goofing off, then why did you hire them in the first place? Let me give you two examples. I worked for somebody who obviously did not trust the people he hired.

We had the worst hurricane heading our way in the history of New York City. And he was at his nice, palatial weekend home in Bermuda. So he thought, well, what's the big deal for him? It wasn't a big deal for us. It was life or death. And he expected us to come to the office even though we would be risking our lives to do so. A client I had who was the CEO of a rather substantial pharmaceutical company, I asked him, I said, what are the hours you expect your people to put in at the office? And he kind of looked at me like I was crazy from the I really don't care. I don't care when they come in. I don't care when they go home. All I care about is they doing the work.

And that should always be the attitude of any boss at any company. And if you're coaching them, you should want them to have that outlook in terms of work, in terms of hiring, in terms of getting things done. So the question is, you know, are they goofing off at home? Are they doing, you know, playing around? Are they eating when they should be working? The question is, you should trust them. You should only hire people who you believe will get stuff done, no matter whether it's 9:00 to 5:00 or 5:00 a.m. to 9:00 p.m. it doesn't matter. Trust them. If you don't, they should get new people.

Time Is Your Biggest Enemy

What are the biggest challenges you'll have as a coach to folks in management and what are their biggest obstacles to success? They could argue that the economy could be a pandemic. It could be the competition, underfunding and lack of good personnel to work with all sorts of things. The one thing that is the biggest challenge to virtually all of us is time. Once time has been spent, we can never get it back. So as a coach, a very important chapter that you can give to the people you work with is how they spend their time. What are they prioritizing their time for? What are their lists of must dos? One, two, three, four.

What can they delegate? What can they put off till another time? Sometimes procrastination is the right thing with something that's not that important. People who have to have control can never delegate. People who have to have control can never say, oh, this isn't that important. They think everything is important and they are not. So again, when you're coaching somebody, look at the way they spend their time, look at the way they waste time and help them to prioritize the one thing that challenges virtually all of us.

Don't Be Too Much Of A People Pleaser

Great networkers are people pleasers for sure. Just don't overdo it. We all like to get compliments. We all want approval from others, but make sure it's for the real reason. Don't make up some image of yourself. Don't try to turn yourself into something just to get the good approval of others because they'll sense it.

And if they've got any kind of power, they'll want no part of that person that you're presenting. If you're being real, if you're being genuine, if you're being a giver and not a taker, people will be attracted to you every time you do something just for the approval of others or just to keep their disapproval away.

It chips away at your self worth, your self esteem. And again, power. People will want no part of you. So be real, be a giver and make sure that you are the real thing when you're connecting to others.

11 Empowering Questions To Ask Yourself (And What Not To Ask)

Rich Litvin is a really smart guy. Go online, take a look at his chapters and read his book. It's called The Prosperous Coach. Even if you're not a coach, you're going to get a lot out of that book, I promise you. I certainly have. Rich came up with 11 questions you should ask yourself as opposed to the ones you should not. So let me give you his list of 11 questions. Ask How can I grow from my mistakes? Not how can I make safer decisions. Number two, how can I be more creative? How can I be more productive? Good creativity leads to better productivity. Number three How can I make more profit? How can I make more revenue? Number four: how can I work less? How can I work more? Interesting distinction.

Five How can I create clients who inspire me? Not How can I inspire more clients? Number six How can I create more leaders? How can I create more followers? Number seven asks How do I implement my idea? Not how do I perfect my idea. Number eight Who can I serve today? How can I sell my coaching? And again, it could be any service or business or product that you control that you're in. Don't just get stuck on the coaching part of it. What tiny steps can I take? How can I feel more confident? Little steps. Little victories lead to greater confidence. That's my interpretation of that. How can I promote my clients' success? How can I promote my business? And finally, how much value can I create? Not how much I should charge. Again, these are really smart things. If you want to get the whole list, I'm happy to send it to you.

What's The One Thing You Can Do To Be Better?

Here's a question I think all bosses should ask all their employees, even their high performing people. Is there one thing, just one thing you could do to be even better at your job? Now why do I like this question? Number one is it's not overwhelming. I'm not telling you to come up with 10 things or 15 things or 20 things to be better. Just one thing, one thing at a time. It's not overwhelming. It's not, Oh my god, I don't know if I could do all those things. You're focusing on one thing at a time. It's like bite size pieces of getting better at your job, and all of us can be better. So even the people who you think are the best in your company, even they could use improvement.

And again, when they come up with their own answer about the one thing they can do to be even better at whatever they do, they're empowering themselves. They're coming up with their answers, not yours. I think it's exciting. I think people will feel encouraged to take on one task at a time to get better without the feeling that they've got a mountain of things they've got to do to get better. So try it with you, people, all of them, those who need a lot of help and those who are even your top people. See what the results are. I think you'd be surprised.

Outstanding Tips For Job Interviews

Who is your prospective employer? Obviously, you're going to go online and do a deep dive into who they are, what they stand for, what they believe in, what's their history, where are they heading? What markets are they looking to go into? Who are their competitors? Are they better than the competition or is it the other way around? By the way, who is interviewing you? You never know you. Perhaps you have something in common with that person. May have gone to the same college or you lived in the same city. Can't hurt to find out. Be creative when you're finding out something about the company. Does a tab at the top of every Google search have news?

So hit that and find out what journalists are saying about the company and what's the investment community? What are they? What are they written about this individual corporation? What are their competitors saying? What are their critics saying? Go to Glassdoor and see what past and current employees are saying about them. These will give you all kinds of hints about who they are and where they're going and what they stand for. Now, a lot of times in a job interview, you're going to be asked. So tell me something about yourself. Well, the one thing you should not do is to repeat what's already on your resume. Talk about something interesting that happened in your life.

Perhaps you climbed Mount Kilimanjaro and you heard it, and found out a great chapter about adversity. Or maybe you led your college basketball team to the league championship and there were valuable chapters about leadership. Or maybe somebody gave you some great advice that really made an impact on your life. Tell them something about you, something that you achieve, something that you accomplish, or some difficult obstacle you had in your life and how you overcame it. These will help them to give you a fuller picture of who you are and the kind of individual that they might want to hire.

How To Succeed In A Virtual Job Interview

Increasingly, prospective employers are going to want to do interviews via Skype or Zoom or similar modalities, maybe in your job you're going to be working from home or some other remote location, and you're going to have to be comfortable seeing and working with clients and colleagues on screen instead of face to face in the same room. And the format for these interviews is pretty similar. You've got to do a deep dive into the company, find out who they are, where they're heading, what they stand for, what they believe, what their products and services are, who are their competitors. You may want to find out some things about the person who is interviewing you. You never know. It might come in handy in the Book of your conversation with that person. Some technical suggestions.

Number one is make sure your laptop or your tablet is fully charged. You do not want to run out of juice in the middle of the interview. Have your cell phone by your side in silence with the phone number of the individual who's going to be interviewing you. If something happens, if there's a technical issue, if you lose the line or whatever, you can easily call them. And at the very least, you can continue the conversation by phone. What else? Make sure your lighting is reflecting on you very nicely, very complementary. You don't have to spend a lot of money on lighting. There is something called Loom Cube there online. You can see them for, again, less than one hundred dollars. You can get a nice light that you can put on the back of your computer in the Book of a conversation online.

It's very helpful and it can hurt and it's not very expensive. Get a microphone if you can. I got this one online, I think for seventy nine dollars at Amazon. There are probably some other online vendors who sell them as well. You get it, it enhances your voice and makes you sound more professional. So I would suggest that as well. Your background should be neutral. Pretty much like my background is here. A lot of times we use a bookcase as a background, which is OK, except if the books are too close to the camera, the interviewer is going to start reading the titles of your books instead of focusing on you. So again, the attention should be on you with a neutral background. They're often going to ask you. So tell me something about yourself.

And again, that's an opportunity not to repeat what's already on your resume, but rather to talk about some big achievement, maybe even in your personal life or some obstacle in life that you overcame. It gives them some insight into who you are and the kind of person you are and your character, which I think is going to be very helpful in making the decision about whether or not to hire you. Very often you'll be asked. So do you have any questions for me about the company? And here are some suggested questions. Number one is where do you think the company is going to be five years from now? It shows curiosity. It shows interest in the company. How will my specific skills help the company achieve its goals? Get your demonstrating to them how you want to help them, that you are there for them. It's not about you, it's about them.

Never forget that. Some other questions and other things you could ask them. What do you wish people knew about the company that they don't know now? Or conversely, what's the biggest misconception people have about the company? When I say people, I mean investors, I mean customers, the media, maybe even employees. So again, it shows curiosity and interest on your part and again, how you can help them again. Be prepared, do your homework on the company and the person you're talking to. I promise you, you're going to feel comfortable and confident no matter what the medium is, even if it's this.

One Last Chance to Make This Book Better for Your Permanent

OK, I admit it, I'm a hypocrite. I ask for reviews. I don't always leave reviews. I say, Well, you know, I'm so important. I'm in a rush. Let me just finish the Book and forget the reviews. Well, I feel for you. I've been there, but I'm telling you, I really need you to leave a written review of this Book. Let me know what you think. What did you like? What could be better? That's how this Book will improve. Now, the beauty of online Books is they're not like books where you just print it. That's it. It never changes. This Book changes constantly. It's updated. We add things. We take things out that you could probably see. I got less hair than some of the earlier chapters in this Book. That's because this chapter is new. We're always updating that I might not look prettier, but we are trying to make this Book look prettier and be better for you.

So I'm asking, please leave a written review and don't just leave a star. No, actually leave several sentences. Let me know what you took away from this Book. How did it help you or not help you give as many details as possible? That's the only way I can make this Book better for you. And hey, since you now have lifetime access to this Book, the Book is going to get better for you too. So please don't just fast forward. Leave a review right now if you've already left a review. You can always hit the edit button at the top right hand portion of your screen, and you can leave a more detailed review. Thanks so much. I really do appreciate it.

7 Elements Of Powerful Communications

Ninety percent of our conversation, 90 percent is with ourselves, the moment that we wake up in the morning, we sort of stumble to the kitchen and start the coffeemaker or put water on for tea. We are beginning that inner dialogue, that inner conversation with ourselves that doesn't end until we go to sleep. And maybe even when we're asleep, we're still talking to ourselves in our dreams. And because of that conversation, we know we understand ourselves perfectly. One hundred percent. I don't need anybody to tell me what I say because I understand. And that's the biggest problem we have in business communication and in personal communication because we understand ourselves so well.

We make the bad assumption, the worst assumption you can make in any kind of communication that others understand us. Let me give you an example from my personal life. Nobody in the world knows me better than my wife. She knows me exceedingly well. And I like to believe the other way around is just as true. And yet there are times that I know when I have said something to her that she did not understand. Well, the responsibility is on me to explain to her, to make sure that I am being clear to her. It's not her job to try to figure out what I'm trying to tell her. And so in the business world, honestly, we're dealing with relative strangers, sometimes absolute strangers.

You've never met this person before in your life and suddenly you've got to communicate with that individual. So to that end, I'd like to offer you, if I can, seven elements of persuasive, clear and powerful communications. It's not what you say, it's what they hear: a man much smarter than I am came up with that line, but I borrowed it from him, if I may. What does that mean? It means that you must constantly be the translator and interpreter of yourself. If we agree that not everybody necessarily understands what we're saying, then you have to go out of your way. Take that first, second, third, fourth step to make sure that others understand you.

So how do you do that if you make one of your compelling, important messages, as we spoke of in point number two, you should follow it up with something like this. Here's what I mean by that. In other words, you're saying the same thing, but in a different way. So you're giving them another way of understanding what you're talking about. Or you can say, here's why I think this is important to you or here's why this changes things, or here's how I came to this conclusion. Or perhaps the best thing you can say is here's an example of what I'm talking about. You're constantly interpreting and translating, you're not taking it for granted that they totally understand what you're saying.

Another technique along these lines is to ask and answer your own questions, because not everybody feels comfortable asking questions. You know, they're thinking about questions. They may not even agree with you, but they may feel others may judge me by the question. Then it might ask. They may feel that what I'm saying is stupid or wrong or incorrect or whatever. So do the favor to them and ask and answer your own questions so you can say something like, if I were you, if I was sitting where you're sitting, here's what I'd want to know or knowing your situation as I do. Here's probably what you're thinking to yourself. You're like getting into their head. And one of the things that we all like in life, we all are connected by this that is being understood, that is being recognized.

And when you ask and answer your own question, you are connecting with them on a very deep and personal level. And it also may encourage them to say, OK, well, I have some more questions. I'm going to start following up what you just said with more questions. Let's say hypothetically, there's bad news about your company or bad news about you. Well, because of this highly connected world that we live in, Internet, social media, et cetera, they probably know it. Assume that they do know it. So bring it up before they do. One reason is because it shows that you're a courageous person. You're not afraid to face controversy, stare it in the eye and bring it on. And number two, you get to talk about it in a way that you want to talk about it. It's like you're setting the stage your way, not their way.

And you could start by saying, you know, you probably know this about our company, but we had a shortfall in our profits this last quarter. Let me tell you why that happened and why we think we're taking the right steps to correct that. So, again, you're bringing it up, but you're also showing how you're handling it. Now, I know everybody here is in the business world and you think, well, feelings and feelings, the business world, we deal with data, we do with analysis, we do with facts, all of which is true. But J.P. Morgan, the great financier from the 19th century, said that we all do virtually anything important in life for one of two reasons. The good reasons and the real reasons. The good reasons are the factual reasons that are unassailable true.

They're 100 percent true. The real reasons or the emotional reasons. And I would argue that we make a vast amount of our decisions in life for how we feel about something, not how we think about something. So let me give you an example. We have a lot of things in common in this room. But one thing we absolutely have in common. One hundred percent absolutely. Is that we're all wearing clothes? Right. That roller in clothes. Why do we wear clothes? Well, it's chilly outside. It was raining earlier today. Maybe it's still raining now. Clothes keep us warm. They keep us dry. And that's a good thing. We could all agree. That is absolutely true. Unassailable truth. Second reason we wear clothes is that we have a social contract in our culture, in our societies, that we don't walk out of the house naked.

We wear clothes to cover certain parts of our body. Am I correct about when we go to the beach? Probably we wear clothing to cover certain parts of our body. That is absolutely true. But if that were the only reason, the only reason we wore clothes, we could spend a minimal amount of money that would keep us warm and dry and protect our modesty. But we don't do it. We spend an inordinate amount of money because of emotional reasons. We buy clothes, we buy clothes because of how they make us feel and how we want others to feel. Look what I have here. I have a necktie. It neither keeps me warm in the cold weather and it doesn't protect my modesty. The tie is not that long, ladies and gentlemen.

So I wear it. It's decorative. I kind of like the way it looks. You wear a business suit because it has a certain formality. It feels like, OK, we're here to talk about business. It's just that some people exude power control. People wear clothes that are kind of sexy because that's the kind of feeling they want others to have about them. Artistic, grungy, funky, funny. All of that is about clothes. The emotional reason that we buy clothes has made people like Giorgio Armani, the Versace family, sand of cocaine, even filthy rich, because they know that we're willing to invest a lot of money because of the emotional attachment that we have to clothes.

Charisma Is Overrated

When it comes to networking, charisma is overrated. What do I mean by charisma? These are people who are outgoing. They're the life of the party. They always have something interesting and witty to say. They're like magnets for people. If you're that way, hey, that's great. Most of us are not. What you can be is present for the person you're talking to, really listening intently, asking smart, relevant questions about what they just said. That person that you're talking to is going to say to themselves, hey, this person cares about me. This person is here for me. This person is present for me. And they're going to be willing to connect with you in a meaningful, purposeful way that will help both of you.

Presence can be learned. Charisma can be learned. Maybe it can. But you can learn to be present, to ask smart questions and to really pay attention. Look, there are people who are successful, who are charismatic, Barack Obama, Bill Clinton, even Donald Trump. But again, most of us are not that way. It can work for you that you're not so charismatic because people will say, I'm not intimidated by this person. I can identify with who he or she really is. So, again, be present, be there, pay attention, ask smart, relevant questions.

How Do Get Funding For Your New Business

When you're thinking about approaching a venture capitalist, a funder for money for your new startup, put yourself in their shoes, answer the kinds of questions that you believe they're going to have for you. So, for example, you need to explain your product or service in such a way that they say, yeah, I get it, I understand it. You might want to do it in the form of a story. How did you come up with this idea? Was there an epiphany? Was there that aha moment where you said to yourself, wow, this is something this is a product or service that I think I can help people with. It's good to explain it in the form of a story because why people understand stories when they hear a story, it's like a screen goes up in their mind.

see the whole scenario being played out. If they really connect with the story that you're telling and the added benefit of a wonderful story is it sticks to the stories. Stay with us. There were stories that you were told as a child that I'm sure you remember today. So please do not underestimate the power of a story. Can you make money? When will you make money, not only for your business, but also and this is important for the venture capitalists. When can they expect to get their investment returned and also get a profit on that investment? One thing you need to be an expert on is being empathetic with your potential customer. You have to see life from their point of view.

What are their fears, their anxieties, their challenges in life or in business, their hopes, their dreams, their aspirations. When you see life from their point of view and you can connect your product or your service to who they are and what they care about, you'll be going a long way to having a really successful product. Is your customer a repeat customer, at least potentially. In other words, if are you selling a subscription service like razor blades, hair color, coffee, something that they might order on a regular basis? If you're not, that's OK. That doesn't necessarily mean you have a bad business by any means. Just be clear to your funder about what kind of a business it is. Who were you? They really want to know the answer to that.

Do you have the track record, the background to make sure that you can at least have the potential of creating a successful business? Have you ever started up a business before? Do you understand manufacturing, if it's a product or marketing or customer service, if they have any doubt about that, or do you have any doubt about that yet? A partner or partners who can help answer these kinds of questions? I guarantee they're going to have value. They have to trust you. This is a long term relationship. This isn't about giving somebody money and saying, that's it, goodbye and good luck. They want to have a relationship with you. That goes on for quite some time, you know, creating a great idea.

That's the easy part. Selling to strangers. That is really tough. By the way, this is not an all inclusive list of every question that you might get from a venture capitalist or a funder. But these are some of the basics. And if you need to keep these in mind, here's a tip for you. Go online and research the people you're going to be pitching to or the company that they represent or more than likely, both see who they are, what is their track record, what are the kinds of companies that they are interested in funding? And if they list and they probably will, companies that they have underwritten in the past call those companies up. If they gave money to the X, Y, Z widget company, great call X, Y, Z and say, hey, listen, I'm interested in the kinds of questions they asked you in the context of your pitch.

And once you reach a deal with them, what would they like to deal with? Were they encouraging that with a hands off? Do they give you some advice? Do they give you connections in context that were helpful for your business? Again, find out a lot about them when you go to Google. Here's another good tip. You'll see you put in a search for these funders at the top of every Google search, there is a tab that says news. Go to that tab and click on it, because that will give you a lot of realistic journalistic stories. About them, that hopefully will give you the good news and bad news about them. So I think it's really important to get an objective point of view if you can find anybody else who knows anything about these folks that you're trying to get money from. Talk to them, please.

Please talk to them. OK, what else are they going to ask you? Where is your product going to be manufactured? Is it going to be in Asia? Is it going to be in North America or is it going to be in the Caribbean? Ask where they're going to ask you where the product is going to be taken off the ground. They might want to follow up with. Are there any tariff issues? Are there any duty issues that you might encounter? Do your homework, do your due diligence on your own business? How much will it cost to make your product what you retail it for? What do you think the valuation is for your product? And how did you come to that figure? Why now? What's the urgency for your business? You know, talk about what's going on in the world, talk about maybe the economy in the world, talk about the culture in the world, trends in the world that might fit and might be relevant for what you are talking about.

Your presentation should be more about showing them things about your product than telling them. What do I mean by that? I was asked by a startup to consult with them about their pitch to venture capital. What their product was, was a brand new cookie, and they wanted to enter the North American market with that cookie. Actually, the cookie was from France, which is perfectly fine. And what they're going to do is talk about the cookie in a chapter as well. And at the end of the presentation, they were going to pass around a plate of cookies to the venture capitalists that they were pitching to. I said, that's great. All sounds good. Here's a suggestion.

Bring in a portable oven and a premade batch mix of some of the cookies. Bake the cookies while you're pitching. Let them smell. Let them take in the aroma of the cookies and let them sort of salivate as they're listening to you. It worked. They got their money. And I see the same thing to you. If there's any way to demonstrate the value of your product, it could be with a chapter. It could be with some sort of animation. It will help you a lot. Should you use PowerPoint? Yes. If it, in fact illustrates the points you were making. If you've got chapters that are overloaded with a lot of statistics or tiny little graphs that can't be possibly understood, then don't do it. Illustrating what you're talking about rather than talking about it in terms of a lot of verbiage in your chapter, I was asked by the CEO of the six biggest insurance companies in the United States to watch him do a pitch to investors from Wall Street. And he wanted me to assess how he did. And so I did.

And so his chapters, again, were loaded with these tiny little graphs, lots of statistics, lots of data. It was impossible to understand. And so he said to me at the end, how do you think I did? I said, look, maybe I'm not that smart. Either I can listen to you or read your chapters. I can't do both. And that's the chapter to you again, use chapters to illustrate your point. You may have heard of the great venture capitalist Guy Kawasaki. Guy has also written some wonderful books about how to pitch to VCs. And Guy has this rule. He calls it the ten, twenty thirty rule. That is ten chapters, no more than ten chapters, no longer than twenty minutes in your pitch and your print point on your chapters should be no smaller than thirty points. Now you may be thinking to yourself ten chapters.

Sounds like two little twenty minutes. I'm not sure we can fit all in twenty minutes. Maybe you're right, maybe you're right. But I think Guy's point is to be a really tough editor. Do not overwhelm your audience. In this case the voices with too much information. If you have forty or sixty chapters in your deck, they will have PowerPoint for TV, and will be overwhelmed. They just will not be able to remember or absorb the information that you're trying to give. If you speak too long, for example, usually an hour is allocated for a pitch. Twenty minutes. Forty minutes for Q&A and. Q&A is really important. I'll get to that in a moment, but you go for 30 or

40 minutes or forty five minutes in your pitch, they don't have enough time to ask you questions at the Q&A.

Part is vitally important. Ladies and gentlemen, I want to know what you're made of. Can you answer the kinds of tough questions that they're going to have for you? And I really think you've got to be prepared for that. But so 20 minutes, I think is OK, we want to do it. Twenty five minutes of a presentation. That's fine, but don't go a real long time. One of the tips, do not give written material to the voices before your presentation, because all they'll be doing during your pitch is looking at your writing. If you want to leave material behind after you're done, that's perfectly OK. Another tip, please practice, practice, practice your presentation. Put a smartphone in front of you, give your pitch, do it over and over and over again until you are happy with it.

To you say to yourself, this is about as good as it can get. You want to show it to somebody you trust, somebody whose judgment you believe in. That's fine, too. I'm often asked, when is it a good time to pitch a new business, and I say any time is a good time to pitch a good business in the most economically challenging times of our history. Companies like Disney, Hewlett-Packard and Uber successfully won money from startup folks, from venture capitalists. So come up with a brilliant idea. Explain it perfectly and execute it brilliantly. I wish you all the success in your new venture.

Bad Assumptions Can Kill A Great Business Relationship

It should be painfully obvious that we should not make assumptions about people based on superficial things like race, gender, ethnicity or age, but yet we still do and it stops us from making great network connections. Same thing about tired old ideas that are way beyond their expiration point. Let me give an example. In the advertising world, they still believe that you could only sell a product to somebody who is between the ages of 18 and forty nine. The belief is that if you're over forty nine and I certainly am, you can't change your mind from one toothpaste to the other toothpaste. Well, in my own life, my wife and I go on different vacations every year.

I've changed the line of my clothing choices often and I used to be a PC user. Now I use Apple products. So believe me, those old rules should be tossed out, especially if you're looking to connect with somebody to make a meaningful network for yourself and for the person that you're talking to. Speaking of talking to them again, we make the foolish assumption that people understand us and that can turn off a potential networking relationship. I don't know about you, but like me, I get up in the morning, I stumble to the kitchen, and start the coffee. But I'm also beginning that internal dialogue that does not end until later that night. When I go to sleep, I understand myself perfectly.

The foolish assumption that I would make is that others understand me as well, and that would be a very dumb idea on my part. So you should always follow the important statements with things like here's what I mean by that. Here's an example of what I'm talking about. Here's how I came to this conclusion. Here's why. But I think this means for the future, again, you're giving an explanation to what you just said that will solidify any great potential networking relationship. Be clear, be understandable, and toss out old rules about assumptions.

Be The Bearer Of Your Own Bad News

Be the bearer of your own bad news, to say the least. We live in a highly connected world and there may be some negative things online and social media about you. If it's something small and not very big, ignore it. But if it's a big accusation and you did not do it, you need to bring it up before your perspective. Networking partner does take charge of the situation. You'll be seen as a stand up person who's not passive. Again, if the charge is incorrect, the story is a bunch of bull, then state your case. And if there's anybody else or anything else that can verify what you're saying, bring that into the conversation as well, that if you did screw up and we all make mistakes, own up to it, don't rationalize it or justify it, said, yes, I made a mistake. Here's what happened.

Put it in context. Here's what I did. I apologize to the person that I wronged. I took some steps to make sure that it does not happen again and to show that I was contrite about what I did. And again, you're showing that you're a mature person, that you're not somebody who hides from things that are being said about you online and that you're you're you're in charge of your life, in charge of your reputation as well. Now, your prospective partner may have questions for you about the situation. Fine. Take as many questions as that person has answered them fully and honestly. Again, be the bearer of your own bad news.

What Is Your Company's Purpose?

What is my company, my product, our services, or our cause really about? You need to be clear in your head about what you do and how you can benefit your customers and your clients. What problems do I solve? You know, honestly, a lot of customers will come to you because they say we have a problem. We want to be more profitable. We want to have a bigger customer base. We want to reach out to new markets. Okay, great. Now you understand their problems and possibly how you can solve them for them. Therefore, that's why you're in business. That's why you're there is to help them to have a more profitable, better business or happier, healthier life. You need to get into the head of your customers. And you do that by asking a lot of smart, relevant, insightful questions and then listen to their answers.

Really, really listen without judgment. Be open minded. You're not there to say, Oh, how much smarter you are, or they shouldn't say this. Just be not a good listener, be a great listener, and watch their tone and body language as they are speaking. Their tone may be kind of down, not very enthusiastic, not very excited. Their body language again may be some sort of scrunched over the words may be right, but the tone and body language are not. I would say listen to the tone. Watch the body language. That is a more truthful interpretation of what they really mean and where they're really at. And finally, you have to answer their unasked but highly important question: Why should I care? What's in it for me? How are you in some meaningful, purposeful, tangible way going to make my life or our business better?

The Business Benefits Of Being A Smart Observer

There are real business benefits for being an outstanding observer of people. Listen to people, listen to their words, and just as importantly, listen to the emotion and the feelings behind the words. Are they excited? Are they angry? Are they energized? Are they happy about something? Really? Really. Listen, with not only your two words, but really with a third ear. I also like to ask open-ended questions to people to begin to learn something about them that might be helpful to me. So one of my favorite questions is what do you wish people knew about you that they don't? Or conversely, what's the biggest misconception people have about you now? When I say people that could be customers, it could be investors, it could be the board of directors, it could be family, friends, employees, anyone.

What do you wish people knew about you that they don't? What's the biggest misconception people have about you? Another question I like to ask people usually at a cocktail party or dinner party, somebody I don't know, I've just met and eventually you get around to that question. So what do you do? They say, Well, I'm a lawyer or a doctor, an engineer or entrepreneur. I say, Oh, interesting. So do you like being a lawyer? I'm telling it, 99% of the time they tell me, No, I don't. I used to. I don't anymore. Oh, that's interesting. So if you could do anything, anything for a living, whether you're qualified for it or not, whether you have the education, the training, the skills, whatever, what would you do? And their answer usually isn't something crazy.

It isn't something wacky. It's not like I want to be quarterback of the Dallas Cowboys or prime minister of India. It's something that's real and I always follow up with. So what's stopping you in their answer and the way they answer? Again, the emotion and the feelings behind it will reveal a lot about them. It's valuable information if you want them as a customer, as a networking partner, as an investor in your business. Again, listen, really, really listen not only to the words, but the emotions behind them.

Power Sales Tips

Here are some of my ideas about how to be an effective and successful sales person. Number one is never underestimate the importance emotions play in the sales process. Let me give you some examples. All of us have something in common. We all wear clothes. Why do we wear clothes? Well, the factual correct reason why we wear clothes is because clothes protect us from the elements. They shield us from the cold, the rain, the sun, the heat, the wind, whatever. They protect us. We also have a social contract that we don't leave the house naked. We cover our bodies with clothes. But if those were the only reasons in the world why we need to close, we would need to spend a lot of money on them. And yet the opposite is true.

We have an emotional connection to the messages that clothes send us and to the rest of the world. I am sexy, I'm powerful, I'm artsy, I'm grungy. Those are emotional attachments that we have with our clothes. Same thing goes for cars. If you had two cars both in the same place, one is very expensive. Let's say it's a Rolls Royce and the other one is a Prius. Not the cheapest car in the world, but far less expensive than that. Rolls Royce. And they 're going to go from point A to point B. They both get there probably more than likely at the same time. But emotionally, they have different attachments. The expensive role says, I am important, I'm powerful, I'm wealthy, I've made it. The Prius says I care about the world. I care about the environment. I'm a good person.

And yet again, if we're just looking for the basics of what a car does, gets us from point A to point B, they both function the same. One costs a lot more than the other. Same goes for houses. If again, the basic function of a house is to put a roof over our heads so we have protection again from the elements and we're comfortable. But really we spend a lot of money on the way a house looks, its location, its situation, the way we decorate it, the grounds around it, and our landscaping. And that's good too. But that, again, is the emotional connection we have to our house. There's no place like home as the old expression goes. And again, that's the emotional part of the sales presentation.

For a home. Now you may be thinking to yourself, Oh, that's all fine and good, but I don't. I don't sell a product that has a lot of emotion to it. I sell screwdrivers or hammers or nails. Nothing very sexy about those. That will only be true. But that means that your customer may be investing emotions in you. How do they feel about you? Do they trust you? Do they believe you? Do they think and know that you are looking out for their best interests, that this is not just a transactional relationship, that really this is something where you just care about them as more than just a customer? One of the most important attributes, anyone in sales, anyone in business, and I would argue anyone in life can have is empathy.

Do you understand where people are coming from? Do you see life from their perspective, their wants, their needs, their desires, their challenges, their fears, their anxieties? When you truly get where they're coming from, where they're at, then you can customize your presentation, your pitch, so it's just right for them. You can say, Here's how my product or my service will in some way benefit your life because I see where you're coming from. Now. The one thing the empathetic person never does is to be judgmental of others. Empathy is not necessarily. It is seeing life from their perspective, walking in their shoes. So that's again, connecting what you're selling to who they are as a person. Great salespeople are great listeners when they're talking about their problems.

Really, really pay attention. And a great listener asks, really smart, relevant, interesting follow up questions. So the person who is doing the talking, in other words, your client, your customer says to him or herself, Wow, this person is really, really listening to me. And never underestimate the importance people play on being heard and being seen. And as a great listener, you are fulfilling those needs. And again, listen, without judgment, you're not there to be some moral superior person to your prospect or your client. You're just there to listen and see how in some way your product or your service can help them in some meaningful way.

Give your customer something extra, something that they really don't expect, something that goes beyond what is normally expected in this kind of a situation. So, for example, a car salesman may say for the first three years that you own or lease this car, there is no charge for servicing or we give you extra accessories in your car that nobody else does. Again, it's something people actually appreciate. Let me tell you something from my own practice as a media and presentation trainer and also as a coach for people just like yourself. At the end of every training that I do, and it's usually with a group of people, I say to them and I see that our relationship does not end now. In fact, in many ways it's just the beginning.

At some point you're going to have to make a presentation in front of an audience. You're going to have to be interviewed by somebody in the media and before those events. Call me with no extra charge. Absolutely. For free. Let's go over your speech. Let's go over your answers that you might give to a reporter. Let's again, fine tune your messaging, because my investment is for them to be really successful in what they do, because the more successful they are, the more that they will refer me to their friends and colleagues and say, Listen, you need to talk to me about your situation. Make sure that the people you are talking to understand you. We overestimate how clear we are in our communication to those that you're trying to reach.

So let me give you some examples from my own life. When I get up in the morning, I sort of stumble to the kitchen. I turn the light on, start the coffee and feed my pets. But what I'm also doing is beginning that internal dialogue that does not end until I go to sleep later that night. Now I understand myself perfectly. I don't need a translator for me. But the mistake that I would make is assuming that. Others understand me. So therefore, it is incumbent upon all of us to interpret and translate what we're saying. So when you make an important statement to a client, you should follow it up with. Here's what I mean by that. Here's an example of what I'm talking about.

Here's how we believe this changes our understanding about whatever you're talking about, or here's how we came to this conclusion. So they're saying to themselves, Ah. Now I understand what he's talking about. Now I understand what he's driving at. Really, really important to tell stories. Lots of them tell stories about clients who are like them, who have benefited in some meaningful way from your product or service. The story will resonate with them. They'll connect to the story, and more importantly, they'll remember it. Its stories, as I always like to say, stick to the brain. And every time you tell a story, it should always finish up with something aspirational. My belief is the three most powerful words in persuasion are Here's what's possible.

In other words, you're connecting your client's imagination to a better life. And you say, If you buy our product or engage in our services, here's what's possible here in some tangible, meaningful way is how your life, your business, your health will be better as a result of what we're offering. Allow people to sample your product or service. There are stores in the United States called Costco or Whole Foods where there are people there who give out samples of food that are being sold in the store. And what they have found up to 30% of the time, if you give somebody a sample of the cheese or the soup or the candy, whatever you're selling, 30% of the time they will convert to by being a buying customer, that's a pretty good deal.

In my own practice, again, the vast majority of the people who come to work with me, my clients come through referral. But occasionally there's somebody who really doesn't know who I am or doesn't know anybody who does know who I am, but they've heard about me and so they're interested. But again, they don't know what it's like to work with me. Say, fine, So let's talk about your issues. Let's talk about your problems. And in that case, they're getting a taste of what it would be like to work with me. And again, the vast majority of the time, they become clients. Should you do PR as part of your sales operation? Yes, But be smart about it. Be strategic about it. We'd all like to have a story about our product or service or company, whatever on the front page of the Wall Street Journal.

Wouldn't that be nice? It's highly unlikely that's going to happen. What could happen is that a blog or a magazine or a podcast that's targeted at the audience you're trying to reach could well be a story about you, your product or your service. So, for example, if you've come up with an interesting software for the banking industry, some blog I'm just making this call financial tech might do a story on you and that is reaching exactly the people you want to get to. And they're far more likely to do a story than the Wall Street Journal. We all make mistakes with our customers. You know, we're all human beings. We all make mistakes. If it's a big mistake, if you really screwed up, explain the mistake and also how you're going to make it up to your customer. How are you going to make good on it? If it's a tiny mistake, like you said, you're going to deliver the product on Tuesday, but it didn't come by Wednesday.

Just a mere apology will do. You don't have to go beyond that. A lot of us have the stereotype, the image that great salespeople are charismatic. Everybody wants to see them, listen to them. They have this great spiel, they have this great conversation pattern, and that's fine. If they do, that's great. There's nothing wrong with that. But let's be honest, most of us are not very charismatic. Most of us are good people, but we don't have that kind of, Oh, I can't stop watching or listening to him or her or something like that. What we can have is presence with our customers and our clients. In other words, being really there for them, paying attention to them, asking smart, incisive, relevant questions about them and their lives so they get the correct impression This person cares about me.

They may not be flashy. They may be. Exciting, but they are present and they care very, very important. Some of us are anxious salespeople. We have a certain anxiety when we're sitting in front of a prospective client, and that's, believe me, far more people than you think. Have that issue reframe what you're talking about. In other words, it's not about you. It's about the product. Focus on the product and what it would mean to that particular client. It's not about you, it's about them. Focus on them and the product and the service and how it will in some way make their lives better and take the focus off of yourself. You are what you sell.

What do I mean by that? Well, let's say I am working out of my gym and I'm thinking about getting a personal trainer, but the personal trainer that I'm seeing is badly out of shape. They're kind of heavy. They're not in good shape or whatever. Well, why did they hire that person? I want somebody who's going to work with me to look really good, to be in tremendous shape. Same thing might go for somebody who sells clothes if they're badly dressed. That's not going to cut it for me. A 26 year old came up to me and said he wanted to be my life coach. Really? I've got ties that are older than that young man. I'm old enough to be his father and then some. Now, if he came to me and said he wants to counsel me and coach me about social communication or about technology, cool.

I'm all ears, but about life coaching, I don't think that's going to happen. If a stockbroker calls me up and says, Hey, I've got some great stock tips for you, well, you must be really rich, Mr. Salesperson of stocks, because unless you are following your own advice, then why are you going to sell me anything? You've got to be wealthy in your own right or I'm not going to be listening to you. You don't have to have a brand new product that no one's ever heard of before. The Wright brothers didn't invent the airplane. Henry Ford didn't invent the car, and Steve Jobs did not invent the personal phone.

But they were all great at enhancing and selling the concepts of the product that they represented them. A lot of folks in my position might say to you, Oh, to be a great salesperson, just be yourself. I say, Be your best self, be empathetic, really listen to your customers, Make an emotional connection between your product and your service and your clients and customers. And when you do that, you'll have a far greater chance of being an incredibly successful salesperson. Thanks so much for reading.

Managerial Skills

And hanging managerial performance, empowering yourself to become a high performance manager, learning decision objectives, how to manage yourself effectively and then manage others, identify the role of SBA head and what is expected of management, how to be a business builder rather than a functional manager supporter after his solution provider for total reasons and its processes. How to be proactive and responsive to current business station situational leadership. The Methodologies of decision, action, learning approach. Sharing real management experience. Total Participation emoluments. His principles keep it short, simple, managing and letting your business during turbulent times.

It is possible or not, what essential things recurred during this period. Are you a leader or a follower? What Mark could say about your business? Do you have a second chance to build your existing business, repair your roof during Sunday, sale through or sell through? Now it's time for you to come up with a template and decide what you want to do next season while learning points. Why do you get to know the real you? Managers don't see themselves objectively to overlook their weakness, overestimate their strength. This lack of awareness and self objectivity, either due to ignorance or neglect, often leads to managerial derailments.

If you should cover your true self now what you want to achieve, identify areas for personal growth and take the necessary action though and change personal confidence, the following exercise can assist you in discovering the real you in your answers to all the exercises. Who are you? What are your positive and negative personality traits? Examples of positive personality traits are being a trustworthy, optimistic person and being disciplined. Examples of negative personality traits are being unreliable, arrogant and pessimistic and being easily irritable. How do you relate to others? Include description of your strengths and weaknesses in personal relationships with superiors, peers and subordinates.

Examples of strengths are being proudly attached to an emphatic example of weaknesses are being selfish, insensitive and being a poor communicator. How do other people perceive you? Are you perceived as being reliable, optimistic, competent, independent, disciplined or friendly? What are your strengths and weaknesses? What are your strengths and weaknesses? What do you really want in life? What does success mean to you? What is your case, really our basic philosophy of life? Do you have a personal mission? If yes, what is it? Do you have clear cut personal and career goals? If yes, what are they writing? Refocus or learn.

Reenergize. Why are you in the mindset? The mind grants power and potential of your mind paradigm to shift the way we see the world in terms of pursuing, understanding, interpreting. We have many, many maps in our head, divided mostly between maps of the way things are released and the way things should be or realize. These maps are indeed conditional. Tolle's words. Action habits, character attitude, personality change, resistance to change the paradigm, change the map and your alter attitudes, behaviors and relationship words to live by shortfalls. They become your words. Watch your words. They become your action, your action. They become your habits. Watch your habits.

They become your character. What your character determines your destiny. Taking into this react language. He makes me so angry. There is nothing I can do just the way I am. I can change. I can. I must practice language. I control my own feelings. Let's look at alternatives. I can choose a different approach. I prefer habits. One does better to physical behaviors, mindset to mind growth, rejecting thoughts to change results, positive thinking, small sailing to success, negative thinking. Life will be like a sinking ship. Fear of false evidence appears real. The surest way to conquer fear is to face it. Change is the only thing Chordettes can't stand. The external environment keeps changing. Experiences are things of the past.

They may not be suitable for the present and the future. For things to change, I must change it myself. My self refers to the way people think about, feel about, add towards a solution. We reach their face and it determines how people see problems. The assumption they make, the way they assess strengths and weaknesses. They are areas of purity. They identify the way they rationalize away problems and justify inaction. The solutions they come up with, the way they go about changing or affecting change. Right then external change you have experienced in the past six months. Right. Five changes you have made to yourself in the past six months. Keep updating. If you come with worries that you are outdated, what will happen? Fourth, challenge categories of change.

They are managing change, categories of performance, internal assessment, external assessment. The seven stage process of managing change. Identify the change step to. And speeding change step one, selling the change, step three, mobilizing resources for change, step for breaking down comfort zones. Step five, reinforcing change success. Step six, continuous learning and change. Step seven. Managing strategic change occurs along nine internal changes into the external environment to enable the organization to combat the art of managing change involves a seven stage process and spreading change encourages companies to keep in close touch with their business environment. The next step is to identify what needs to be changed within the organization.

To enable it to combat the change has to be solved internally to win the commitment of the people involved and affected by it. The first stage involves building a team of people and getting the necessary resources. The company's comfort zone. Our complacency has to be broken down, and a success in implementing change, however small, must be publicized and reinforced. The final stage of change is campaigns, learning and improvements. And errors, so organizational change you first and there are consequences, Khama errors allowing the much complication failing to create is facing slip, powerful, good inoculation, underestimating the power of vision. And they're communicating the vision for meeting obstacles.

The blog, the knee vision, failing to create short term means declaring victory. So neglecting to act or change firmly in corporate culture. Consequences of strategies Arendse implemented well. Acquisition down to you expect synergies.

Reengineering takes too long and costs too much to match my full challenge. The dynamics of change, the dynamics of change. I don't know what the world's going to be. All I know is it is going to be nothing like it is today. It is going to be a force to control your destiny or someone else will. Savan powerful reasons for change change to be events since change to be effective, change to motivate, change to lead, change, the gradual change to survive, change the betterment of all the rationale for change.

Change to the Ephesians means is a necessity for companies in Khampa to do and cost driven industries change to be effective means that companies must provide the right goods and services and do the right things in a fast changing market. Companies need to change the way they motivate people in order to retain employees in the long run to strengthen its competitive position. A company often has to change from being a follower, to being an industry leader to improve and grow. Companies must be willing to go in the direction where growth opportunities lie. Sometimes the only option open to a company in order for it to survive is for it to change with its markets. The most powerful reason for change is the betterment of all decisions to every financial year business, LogMeIn, same Cagle's, Renagel business plan, KEH management plan and action by using for peace in the visual performance area a new way of working behaviors. There are seven and W.

There will be Harriers. They were distilled from the town new way of working statement, which from an important basis for much of the cultural change, imagine group of companies in undergoing how this fits together is shown in the next chapter and WWE statement driven by results, not process in terms of poor performance, assisted by high performers and increasingly passionate about people being stretched limits, empowered to take frontline positions, energized by change and innovation, externally focused and quick to grasp opportunities brave enough to take calculated risk abscessed with the customer world class in teamwork, strategic alliance and joint venture and W-W behaviors. Performance focus. People development, empowerment, change, orientation.

Risk taking, customer focused teamwork. Affirmations every day and in every way I am getting better and better. To me, everything is possible. It is not always until I win on being a manager. The one contribution a manager is uniquely expected to make is to give all the vision and ability to firms who are managers, individuals who are directly responsible for getting work done in an organization with and through other people becoming a manager. Can anyone become a manager? In theory, yes, in practice. And now many people are unable or unwilling. So to the needs of management, how do you become a manager? People are usually paramount for one of the following reasons. They are good at their present job. They have been with the company a long time. Their age gives them seniority. They know the right people.

They happen to be in the right place at the right time. Our day promotions, because they will make good managers. They are all managerial top managers, middle manager, first line manager, basic management levels, and my other managerial functions. Managerial roles, managerial generally perform

Tanzy operations like the interrelates roles, which can be grouped into three basic categories interpersonal roles in developing and maintaining good relationship with magnificent other through interpersonal roles that managers play are those of figurehead leader Lasan informational roles, part receiving and transmitting information manager gather and disseminate information through the three informational roles.

Four of monitor disseminator and spokesperson dilutional roles manager in every organization make innumerous decisions. In the Book of their work, managers play decision making roles. Entire brand new disturbance. Handler, resource allocator and negotiator interpersonal. Real fear had literalism, description, perform symbolic duties of the little or Sergel nature, responsible for motivating a subordinate and for staffing and training, maintain a network of outside contact examples, signing the legal document, greeting visitors most managerial activities involving subordinates, making phone calls, acknowledgments of mail, informational role monitor disseminator spokesperson description, seeks and receives information to understand organization and environment, transmits information to all the members of the organization, transmits information about organization to outsiders, samples, reading periodicals and reports maintained personal contacts providing the Mamas and Papas holding meetings.

Board meeting is handling male positional roles and Trepanier disturbance. Handler resource allocator negotiator. Its corruption and its AIDS and promotes organizational improvement projects takes corrective action when organizations face important, unexpected disturbance. Look, all kinds of resources represent the organization in your negotiation example, identifying new business opportunities, these highly strategic decision solving, interpersonal conflicts and employee grievances, budgeting, scheduling, negotiating business deals, managers, task area, technical people, administration managers, recruitment quicker decision making, greater use of management techniques, more time on communication and consultation, more of information. Keeping up to date has more reading.

Manager's responsibilities, why should a manager be in management observation, identify, collection, compilation, presentation, analyst, blend strategies, implementation improvements, culture. Traditionally, any theories of leadership, meningeal fact of life, one, longhairs, most managers work long hours and working hours tend to increase as one advances the higher managerial observables to fragmentation interruption. Our common managerial work tasks are generally completed quickly. Three operation managers handle a wide variety of issues and activities throughout the day, and important activities are entire pursuits with trivial ones.

For lack of reflective planning, managers aren't reflective planners, main activities are react to in nature. Five oral communication managers generally spend most of their time communicating orally with others. Most of it involves the exchange of information and it seems to influence people, seeking interpersonal contacts. Managers spent little time working alone. They spend most of their time interacting with subordinates, peer superior and other people inside and outside of the organization. Stressful nagging is a tough and highly demanding job, and studies show that they experience stress everyday. It's working managers really highly and networks of internal and external contacts to function effectively, dead vault, considerable effort and time to foster a relationship with others whose cooperation is required in satisfying their emerging agendas.

Organizational politics managers cannot avoid organizational politics. Decision processes are disorderly and national such that decision processes are likely to be characterized more by confusion, disorder and emotionality. That's by Ray Chanty. Information is often resorted to sir press conception about the best Book of action or a self-serving interest in a particular choice. The problem and exit about choosing among technology alternatives may result in denial of negative evidence. Procrastination and panic reaction by managers. Who is a high performance manager, a high performance manager is one who is both effective and efficient in getting things done and throws others effectiveness is the ability to choose appropriate goals and achieve them.

Effectiveness is essentially doing the right things. Ever since he has the ability to make the best of available resources in the process of attaining goals, it is essentially those things, right? In short, a high performance manager does the right things right. How to become a high achiever. Strong leaders estimate achievement, try and model it for the day or people. What is a two month orientation achievement orientation can define as the inner rise or excel or compete against a standard of excellence. General characteristic of high achievers, one ambition's high achievers have a strong desire to achieve something worthwhile. They have a clear sense of purpose and direction.

To focus high achievers exclusively on predetermined goals, three high self-esteem high achievers demonstrate high levels of self-esteem. High self-esteem enables high achievers to stretch their personal limits to perform their personal best for energetic high achievers are energetic with levels else that minimum wage is steered clear of sustain a high or to drive five B is toward action. High achievers are results oriented. They take the initiative to make things happen. Simpler part, I get to make my own breaks. They also dare to take calculated risk. Sig's accomplishments oriented high achievers are most concerned with knowing they have done well down with the real work that success brings. Seven resilient high consumers are persistent and determined in the face of adversity.

They quickly bounce back from setbacks. They persist until they obtain their desired result. So. They see I get yours quickly, sump pump station there in alternative Books of action that terminate the preferred cause and coal miners, their subordinates, what needs to be done next? My team players' paper forms are frequently a collective act like it's yours. Collaborate with others to leverage their lifelong learners. I Get Yours are lifelong learners who subscribe faithfully to the process of continuous improvement. They continually educate themselves and seek new knowledge in their field to maintain the competitive edge they make mistakes as learning. Pakhtun these.

Tough tips on becoming a high achiever inspire others with a compelling vision for an organizational department, social museum and motorways other towers peak performance, the mission should be simple and compelling to the organizational members, set challenging goals and focus on them, establish challenging goals which are as a party with organizational departments of mission. Develop action plans for attending Kyoto goals that are mine specific action with deadlines to attain your goals. For example, what skills or knowledge is required to help you obtain your goals? What personal contacts do you need to establish? What are the potential obstacles which may be encountered and maintained as you are seeing within yourself? Life is truly a self-fulfilling prophecy.

PACY, build up your self-esteem. Get rid of self limiting beliefs. Weaves see them as opportunities and challenges, not problems. Artery visualizes success and practices positive self-talk. Remember that you will never know what you can do until you try to show concern for both people and operations. Show trust and confidence in your subordinates and power, trust and confidence in your subordinates. Empower them with adequate decision making responsibilities and outright seek others. Advice and work related matters maintain persistence. High performance managers are fully aware that success doesn't come easily. Perseverance, in essence, she'll maintain flexibility that quickly and new realities be open to new ideas and learn from others.

Who knows more than you continually that and change your behavior until you attain the desired result. Be this is, you make timely decisions based upon available facts. Don't hesitate to take calculated risk. Remember that being decisive doesn't mean action. Garishly many managers that themselves get wiped down in their decision making, especially those with too much education. Promote teamwork, develop cooperative goals, link the goals of management and those of the employees. Create a Cross Faction team to improve CC business process, break down the permanent barriers and promote participation management. Share relevant or useful information.

Keep track of process, review and monitor progress towards attainment of your goals from time to time. Take corrective action and modify goals if necessary due to changing circumstances. Lead a healthy lifestyle. Maintain physical fitness by exercising and exercise for twenty thirty minutes, three to four times a week, maintain a balanced diet, have adequate sleep and rest. Commit to lifelong learning, continue self development. Acquire the necessary knowledge and skills for attaining your goals.

Be willing to admit mistakes or weaknesses, solicit Hana's and constructive feedback from others regarding your strengths and weaknesses, self esteem, what is self esteem, self-esteem and what relation? Of oneself and either a positive or negative way to entity, own and handle self esteem. Now the real you, what is your inner soul and feeling? What are your strange and weaknesses as perceived by you and others who know you? Well. Where are you headed in life? What does this mean to you? Make a list of what you like about yourself, recognize and appreciate your abilities and positive people train the engineer yourself. I didn't find these cars. Paul's beliefs about yourself say stop or cancel.

Cancel allows when you encounter negative thoughts propagated by your pathological critic instead of thinking about them. Learn to love and accept yourself as you are told gracefully. What you cannot change does not compare yourself unfavorably with others. You are unique. Improve your personal appearance by addressing different laws widely or changing your hairstyle. Let go of perfecting your scene. No one is perfect through the mistakes and failures as a learning experience or stepping stones to subsequent successes. Develop and reflect a positive attitude if I can do it. Never underestimate your abilities. Practice positive self talk, talk about your winners, visualize successes in your career and other aspects of your life.

At step one under the person's responsibility. For your life and make a firm decision to change for the weather, determine your long term and short term goals, goals should be specific, measurable, attainable, relevant to your mission and time bounded based or action of self chosen Mallee's Naziism stances review process, subclause attainment of your goals and take the necessary corrective action. Have faith in God and hope for the best outcome, your fears by doing exactly what you fear, pray or meditate daily, celebrate your accomplishment and success, give yourself credit and don't really attribute your accomplishments to luck associated with high achievers and friends who are nourishing, avoid—Hallie's or toxic people seek mutual benefit in all human interactions by creating one mean relationship.

Treat others as you would like to be treated. Look for the good in people, lead a balanced life and see continual self improvement. Maintain your health through proper nutrition, exercise and sufficient rest. Read at least one new book every month and be open to new ideas. Count your blessings such as good health and a loving sport. Instead of wallowing in self-pity, do something good for others. You will feel good about yourself when you assist others. Never belittle yourself. Sape accomplishments with a tank and a smile. Learn to be assertive. Have the courage to voice your opinions or to start your ledger. They may rise without violating the rights of others.

Say no to unreasonable requests. Ignore and unkind or unjustified comments made by others about you and consumers are often compliments in these pleas are mere manifestation of enemy. Learn to love your job and take pride in your work and change your knowledge and job. Play the skills, become an expert in your own chosen field. Let go of your negative past and look to the future. Maintain personal integrity, honor, all promises and commitments. Self-assessment rating your self-esteem directions read through each of the following statements, but a D for true in the space provided. If a statement is generally true for you, leave the space blank. If it is not true behance in your responses, I allow myself, I tend not to worry about what the future holds.

I can visualize myself doing better in my job career. I don't brag about myself, I can be alone and not feel isolated, I have peace of mind and Imagineer I can admit my mistakes. I always question when I am focused, I am willing to take calculated risk. I don't find fault with other people. I get along well with others. I can make up my mind and stick to it. It is easier to express opinions. I welcome constructive criticism. I feel comfortable receiving and giving compliments. I am. It's easy with strangers. I do what I think is right, even if others don't approve of it. I can express to others my true feelings. I can share with others about my strengths and weaknesses. I feel good about the judgment of others. Persistence.

What persistence is a continuous effort applied to attaining a goal without giving up until you succeed, is hanging on when the odds stacked up against you. But, you know, you are right that this group is also often successful through trial and error or the ability to follow through on an idea long after the mood has passed. The importance of persistence and I think worthwhile has ever been achieved without having the courage to engage it and the persistence to finish it.

Man Intelligent and talented managers have failed to become high achievers due to the lack of persistenced' Antibes on maintaining persistence. Have complete faith in yourself and in God. Do your best and leave the rest to go. Remind yourself daily about the goals to be attained. Execute your action plan daily. The high priority work first associated with positive oriented find friends white—Horlicks are toxic people. Never never. You persist until you succeed. Treat failures as learning experiences or stepping stones to subsequent successes. Be prepared to face the unexpected.

Mainstays, the company of individuals having similar values and goals, assures groups of often helps to maintain one's persistence. But it is professional literature when you are feeling down, predict positive self-talk, and repeat the information regularly. I can do it, Sir Thomas. What is certain, this is standing up for personal rights and expressing those feelings and beliefs in dry times and appropriate ways which don't violate another person's right is certain behaviors often create a swimming station. Assertiveness is being done, firm and respectful in interpersonal relation patterns of behavior. The male characteristic of passive behaviors are giving into other people's requests, not expressing one's feelings or viewpoints honestly and apologizing excessively.

It generally communicates a message of inferiority. Aggressive behavior involves ignoring the rights of older people, blaming others for problems and mistakes, and verbal hostility. And who cares? It communicates an impression of superiority. Aggressive behavior often results in meaning lost. The benefit of assertiveness or fulfilling relationships are all mutual respect. Enhanced communication, reduce personal stress, improves your chances of attaining your goals, exercise personal rights without undue anxiety, and without sacrificing the rights of others and having self-confidence how to refuse unreasonable demands from others. 12 tips on how to become more assertive in the workplace.

Demonstrate self-confidence, stress confidently, speak confidently and act confidently. And you have specific facts to substantiate your statements. Reasonable requests ensure that your demands or requests are reasonable and don't violate the rights of others. You practice expressing your requirements, which are provision and conviction, be firm and polite, and learn to say no firmly and politely to unreasonable requests from others. Stand up for your legitimate rights. Don't apologize excessively as it only distracts from your credibility. State problem. Objectively, use bad language to back up your viewpoint.

Maintaining eye contact, upright posture, straight shoulders and using hand gestures to disburse and use your facial expression are consistent with the intended message that the broken research technique keeps saying what you want over and over again without getting angry. Use the Aveda assertion technique first. Let the other person know that you sympathize with his or her situation. Then state. Will you still expect that person to use I statements to express your true feelings? Example. I feel angry when you don't know your promise. Instead, you always dishonor your promise, reward judgment of the other person's behavior and episodes such as never and always maintain composure.

Keep your cool during a confrontation with others. Focus attention on the needs to solve the problem. This creep, the other person's behavior specially and objectively avoids attending the individual. For example, you might say you, having failed to meet work deadlines twice this month instead of you, are a reliable employee. Take undesirable behavior of subordinates precisely and tactfully point out subordinates clearly and tactfully the consequences of their undesirable behavior at the workplace. Don't hesitate to express your disagreement. When you disagree with someone, you can express your disagreement mightily by raising your eyebrows, looking away, shaking your head, or changing your topic of conversation.

Self-assessment, how smart you are, you ask for A, yes or no, B, harnessing yourself to express your feelings to others in a clear and the harmful fashion of being able to ask your colleagues for assistance are small favors to speak your mind. When you think differently from others, are you able to say no to unreasonable requests? Do you maintain contact when you talk to others? Are you able to stay? Specifically, what bothers you in a tactful manner to ask questions? When you are confused? Do you stand up for your legitimate rights to express anger appropriately? Do you respect the basic rights of other people? S objectivity? Self objectivity is essential in knowing one's own strengths and weaknesses and utilizing the strengths effectively while compensating for weaknesses.

It involves focusing our minds on seeking the truth, not denying painful realities and being unable to name knowledge or feedback from others. And it creates unrealistic leave of oneself based upon facts or hands. Feedback from others necessitates self-awareness, a process by which an individual becomes homeschooled in some aspect of reality related to one's character, feelings and motives. d'Antibes tips on maintaining self objectivity and profiting from its assumed self responsibility. Let go of perfectness. You seem to avoid being defensive from the perspective of feedback practice self disclosure, Konforti said. Assessments instruments compensate for weaknesses. Maintain a journal, form a mastermind alliums. Be a lifelong learner.

Time management. What is time management, time management is actually self-management management, it involves managing yourself in such a manner as to optimize the time you have. The time management metrics important urgent Quadrant one activities project with Diddley's work strike to resolve problems, anger customers, not urgent Quadrant two activities long term planning, networking, training, personal development, not important. Urgent Quadrant three activities, unnecessary meetings, some telephone calls. Dropping visitors, some reports. Not an urgent quadrant for activities, unnecessary socializing, lunch, lunch breaks. Junk mail, some telephone calls, and highly successful managers spend most of their time on activities . What activities in Quadrant three and four minimize activities related to quadrant one.

Come on, time wasters, self assessment. How well do you manage your time? As for a yes or no, be harnessed yourself, though you make it daily to the least. Try to establish specific goals with the lines. Three. Do you do important things? First for the article Challenging task when you are at your best five the you assess socializing sees. Do you keep its eye on long periodically as a means of improving your time use to sound the key priorities correctly organized. A Do you keep your telephone calls business like nine the often needed lies then little jades work that can be done by others. Effective leadership. What is leadership is the process of influencing people to stream willingly and and securely toward the management of the goals.

Top ten eight mile attributes use of Malaysian Leader One Hana's to good communication. Three High self esteem for team player five sportive seas inspiring Selam competent a forward looking nine. This issue has ten achievement oriented types of leadership style. Appropriate leadership style, effective communication, what is communication is a process of sharing meaning between the sender and receiver of a message effective when the message transmitted by the sender is understood perfectly by the receiver may are barriers to effective communication, differing perception, selective perception, Reles judgments, emotions, poor listening, skill in constant verbal and nonverbal communication, information overload, credibility, language difference, parameter lation, six C's of effective written communication, clarity with specific and straightforward use, simple words and short sentences.

Write in the language after either giving the message a little to make the subject clear coziness. The message should be as brief as possible, necessary and necessary words such as. Needless to say, and please be advised that if the message is long, provide a one page summary which clarifies the main points completeness. Provide the necessary information which allows the reader to take necessary action without needing to ask questions . Organize your message in a coherent manner. Break down your message into major points which can then be subdivided into starting point first, limit each paragraph into one main idea which should be reflected in the topic sentence car to see your message should be written in a manner which not only gets your message across, but also promise good real correctness as you're doing it. The message has curated information about getting along well with your subordinates and peers that tips on improving human relations.

With subordinates who get to know a subordinate as an individual, each is different. To give credit where credit is due to be open minded for key subordinates informed of matters that are relevant to their jobs. Five Don't reprimand subordinates in public seats, don't play favorites. Seldom show concern for subordinates growth and self improvement, a focus on the good points in subordinates and let them know they are highly valued nine three subordinates with respect and dignity to have subordinates to overcome job related problems. Townships in Prolene can move relations with peers who share ideas, skills, experiences, information to assist peers in growth and personal development. Three, don't take advantage of their weakness for sympathy for their problems.

Five, below you maintain confidentiality. Six, defend your peers in their absence. Speak positively about seven. Show respect for your peers and be courteous, pleasant and positive in your interaction with your peers. Nine Recognize the accomplishments of your peers, then pass on to other people and compliments paid to your peers by third parties. Method of overcoming resistance to change. Structural change, creating a healthy organizational culture to ensure a continuous flow of quality goods and services, a culture of call to must be woven into the fabric of everyday life strategic management. Suwat Emily's potential internal strengths: a distinctive competence, adequate financial services, good competitive skill, off by buyers and acknowledged market leader well conceived with functional areas.

Strategies of the economies of scale insulated from strong competitive pressures, potential internal weaknesses, no clear strategic direction, absolute personalities, subpar profitability because of lack of managerial depth and skills or competence. Poor track record in implementing strategy. But I agree with internal operation problems piling behind in R&D to narrow our product line potential external opportunities. So. Additional customer groups and our new markets are segments product lines to meet a broader range of customer needs, diversify interrelated products, vertical integration, and fall trade barriers in attractive foreign markets.

Complacency among rival firms, foster market growth. Potential external trees, entry of lower cost foreign competitors, rising sales of substitute products, slower market growth, it was sheathed in foreign exchange rates and trade policies, offering governments costly regulatory requirements, adverse demographic changes, changing by power of customer or suppliers, changing buyer needs. And Tacitus' poor and better statement, Of course. Of course, based on time spent, long range goals spanning more than three years, intermediated change goals spanning between one and three years, short range goals with time span one year or less, types of goals based on breed of influence, corporate goals that apply to the entire organization, divisional goals that apply to certain divisions, sectional goals that apply to certain section, individual goals that apply to certain individual benefits of goals.

ABTA transforms broad measures into specific action. Challenging goals can increase performance and clarify expectations. Nabal measurements of progress towards the statement of organizational mission. Facilitate managers in directing and coordinating the efforts of subordinates as performance, evaluation and control. Effective Organizational Mission Statement Museum Menck Excel Bahouth has a twofold mission for our customers in Malaysia. We will provide reliable, prompt cocktails and in a team banking and related financial service we meet or exceed their requirements for our employees. We will create a positive working environment which promotes teamwork, personal growth and mutual respect.

Corporate values want doing the right things the first time to maintain integrity and trust at all times. Three. Seeking continuous improvement in everything we do for communicating in an open and Hana's manner, five empowering employees and developing their potential cease responding positively to change. Seven, encouraging participative management and aid, promoting innovation and creative problem solving.

www.ingramcontent.com/pod-product-compliance
Lightning Source LLC
Chambersburg PA
CBHW071936210526
45479CB00002B/705
9798329500493